Show me the Way

50 BIBLE STUDY IDEAS FOR YOUTH

Todd Outcalt

Abingdon Press
Nashville

SHOW ME THE WAY: 50 BIBLE STUDY IDEAS FOR YOUTH

This book is printed on acid-free, recycled paper.

ISBN 0-687-09562-X

00 01 02 03 04 05 06 07 08 09—10 9 8 7 6 5 4 3 2 1

MANUFACTURED IN THE UNITED STATES OF AMERICA

Dedication

To Paula

Acknowledgements

I'm grateful, as always, to my friends at Abingdon
who saw the promise in this book.
Special thanks to Tony Peterson, Sheila Hewitt, and
Joy Thompson for their support and editing skills.

I also recognize the help and support
of the many teenagers over the years who have
added to my knowledge and allowed me the joy of
working alongside them. Thanks also to the people
of University Heights United Methodist Church
for their support and prayers.
Grateful thanks also go to Jim and Mina Hale.

Finally, thanks to Becky, Chelsey, and Logan
for offering up a few evenings without Dad
so that I could finish the project.

Contents

Introduction 9

Part One: Creative Teaching 15

Part Two: Bible Learning Games 47

Part Three: Ready-to-Go Retreats & Bible Studies 71

Part Four: Bible Talks & More 85

Introduction

Each year, the number-one selling book in America is the Bible. But did you know that most Bibles are never read? And in spite of our attempts to read and understand the book, the Bible can still seem elusive and difficult. The reasons are many.

First, perhaps the difficulty stems from the fact that the Bible is actually a collection of books—a library of history, poetry, wisdom, gospel, and apocalyptic writing. The Bible contains a sizable amount of information. That fact alone can be humbling. After all, how do we begin to absorb such a massive book?

Second, the Bible is an ancient book. The language, stories, and culture can seem so far removed from our time and place that people sometimes wonder how the Bible can have any relevancy in the modern world.

Finally, the Bible is an important book. Christians have been called "people of the book," and for good reason. The Bible stands alone as the primary revelation of our understanding of God, of Jesus Christ, and of the movement of God in human history. We can get goose bumps and a dry throat when someone asks, "What does the Bible say?"

Perhaps these are the reasons so many people give up on Bible reading and Bible study so easily. So our Bibles gather dust instead of fingerprints.

Experience has shown however, that many teenagers are eager to read and study the Bible. They hear others talking about this book, or they feel an obligation to know more about their own faith. Sometimes their faith compels them to undertake the journey of biblical exploration with a group of friends.

Those who work with teenagers can feel overwhelmed by the questions and concerns youth have about life, love, and the Bible. We want to know what we can do to teach the Bible more effectively to teenagers, but we often feel that we lack the knowledge or the know-how. Some basic concepts can give youth leaders a confidence boost. Keep these concepts in mind as you use this book.

Often when we speak of "learning" or "knowing" the Bible, we are talking about a knowledge of the biblical *text* itself. Learning the Bible is learning the words of the Bible. At least that is what most people have in mind when they speak of knowing the Scriptures. In other words, knowing the Bible is being able to recall the Ten Commandments, the Lord's Prayer as it is found in Luke, or some portion of 1 Corinthians 13.

However, on a practical level, we can see that knowing the Bible in this way can be a daunting and demanding task—especially for those who have difficulty remembering their own phone number or address.

But on another level, we can see that "knowing the Bible" means something else as well. As important as the knowledge of the biblical text may be, that knowledge is only the beginning. We often misunderstand the text if we know nothing of the *context*. In fact, in my work as a pastor, I have come to the conclusion that few people read the Bible with any depth of understanding, especially when we consider the broad sweep of history, the various types of writing found in

Show Me the Way

the Bible, and the cultural aspects of the text. Our lack of understanding in these areas may be a reason so many people give up on reading the Bible. The Scriptures are—even for a seminary-trained person—often hard to comprehend. How much more difficult must the Bible seem to folks who do not have a background in biblical studies, history, languages, and such?

So the second important facet of knowing the Bible is understanding the context.

A third aspect of teaching the Bible to youth has to do with *interpretation*. After we have the text itself and some idea of the context, what does a particular passage mean? What does it tell us about God? And what does the passage have to do with our contemporary situations and needs? What are the implications for our lives?

We could argue that interpretation is the most important aspect of understanding the Bible, for the meaning leads to implications for living. If we do not understand what a text means, how can that text help us comprehend God's desire for us, understand God's grace, or experience God's strength?

The Bible is a difficult book, and comprehension often emerges only after much struggle and study. How are we to interpret, for example, Jesus' command to "pluck out your eye"? What does it mean to "love your neighbor as yourself"? And what, for heaven's sake, does it mean to be "the salt of the earth"? Knowing what the text says will not always help us know what a text means. Interpretation involves prayer, discussion, thought, meditation, and listening to the insights of others. That is why the Bible often gains meaning within the context of the community we call the church.

To illustrate these points, consider the Ten Commandments. Although most Christians would say that these commandments represent one of the most important texts in the Bible, many Christians cannot actually write all ten from memory. Most Christians do not know where in the Bible these commandments are found. This is not an indictment—just an observation.

But beyond the text itself, once we know what the Ten Commandments say ("Have no other gods before me," "Do not murder," "Do not steal," and so forth), we have to ask, Why were these commandments given? When? To whom? When and under what circumstances were they recorded?

Then we ask, What do these commandments mean and what are the implications for our lives? For example, the fourth commandment is, "Remember the sabbath day, and keep it holy" (Exodus 20:8). But what does this mean? What is the sabbath? What constitutes work? Which day is the sabbath (Friday, Saturday, or Sunday)? How do we make this day holy?

Once we have determined meaning, we have the challenge of actually living by the precept. The entire purpose of the Bible is to help us to live for God and others, with the knowledge and compassion that the Scriptures teach.

Knowing the Bible means that the biblical text, the context, and the interpretation lead to implications for living as those who can say, "I believe the Bible."

In this collection of ideas, I have tried to offer a healthy balance in each of these three important areas of Bible study. These ideas are meant to help teenagers grow in their knowledge and joy of the Scriptures. Some ideas are made for teens who have little or no knowledge of the Scriptures. Other ideas can be used with teens who have mastered the basics and are longing for deeper knowledge and understanding. Some ideas will seem trite and insignificant in some youth groups. Other ideas will challenge groups in new ways.

As you read through the various choices in this book, keep in mind the differences I have outlined above.

The Bible's Text

These ideas will help youth learn the text, memorize some of it, and broaden their base of understanding of the actual words of Scripture.

The Bible's Context

These ideas will challenge youth to learn about the historical, social, and other aspects of the text. Some ideas will offer a comprehensive approach to the entire Bible; others will focus on particular books of the Bible or even single verses.

The Bible's Meaning

These ideas will assist youth and their leaders in discussing and learning about the implications of particular verses. The focus will be on helping youth grow in their understanding of what the Scriptures can offer them by way of guidance, devotion, prayer, and growth.

Finally, as you use this book,

I hope that you will also discover something in the teaching of the Bible. That is, in the teaching there can also be much learning. I know that I have grown in my own faith and understanding of God as I have listened to and struggled with youth over the course of many years. Teenagers have something to teach us about this majestic book we call the Bible.

Who knows, after we have used the ideas in this book, we may find that we are closer to God than we ever realized. And maybe . . . just maybe, we will even be able to recite the Ten Commandments from memory!

Show Me the Way

PART ONE

Creative Teaching

The heart of this book beats with a desire to teach the Bible to teenagers. However, as all great teachers can attest, no two pupils learn at the same pace; nor do any two students learn by means of the same techniques and methods. Teaching the Bible, therefore, must be a ministry of creativity and insight. Somewhere, a teacher has to push the right buttons that will enable or inspire a student to learn.

But don't forget: The Bible is a massive book—a collection of 66 books to be more exact—and no student of the Bible will ever mine all of the wealth of the Scriptures in a lifetime.

Creatively teaching the Bible may be more a work of perspiration and persistence rather than expertise. It will never be enough simply to ask teenagers to read the Bible from cover to cover. Such a technique, while well-meaning, will usually result in frustration and resignation. Remember, it's better to give teenagers a bit of the Bible at a time rather than having their Bibles gather dust.

This section of SHOW ME THE WAY provides a multitude of creative teaching methods—each illustrated by a practical lesson that can be readily used in your next meeting. These lessons will help your students not only learn the Bible but also learn about the Bible and from the Bible.

Show Me the Way

1. Now Hear This!

Romans 10:17 states: "So faith comes from what is heard, and what is heard comes through the word of Christ." Learning the Scriptures is often more powerful when the words and lessons are not only read, but heard, absorbed, and repeated.

A simple technique to use with youth is to invite the teenagers to listen to a Bible story, perhaps more than once. Then allow the youth to repeat the story aloud, thereby forming a more lasting memory or impression.

Begin this method by having the teenagers sit in a circle. Read aloud a Bible lesson. Then pass an item such as a sponge ball to the youth on your right. Ask this youth to begin repeating the Bible lesson that he or she just heard. When the youth can remember no more, he or she passes the ball to the next person in the circle, who continues telling the story aloud. Continue around the circle until the story has been told or retold a number of times.

This is a great method to use, especially when teaching Bible narratives (as opposed to poetry, epistles, or quotations). Most teens will pick up a story or parable right away and enjoy telling the story or hearing it from their peers.

2. A Penny for Your Thoughts

This method is a quick and easy way to get youth to reflect on the meaning of a passage of Scripture. This idea will not only help teens remember a Bible passage, but more important, it can help them express what the text means.

Bring a handful of pennies to the meeting or session. Select some Bible passages that you would like to read to the group (these should be as brief as possible).

After reading aloud a Scripture passage, immediately call someone's name and say, "A penny for your thoughts." If that person can offer a quick insight or thought about the Bible passage, give him or her a penny. If there is hesitation or if that person draws a mental blank, quickly call on someone else. Repeat the activity until several insights have been offered.

You may do several Bible passages this way. You might be amazed at how insightful and wise many youth become when you try this technique. It is a non-competitive way to reinforce our need to think about what the Bible says.

Remind the students from time to time that no answer will be considered stupid or incorrect. All opinions and insights count. As this technique demonstrates, learning the Bible can be fun and fast-paced.

3. Bible Biography

One effective method for teaching the Bible is to select a specific biblical personality and follow that person's life and faith, learning from his or her failures and triumphs. Doing a Bible biography can be an exciting venture for teenagers, especially if you focus on some of the more colorful Bible personalities, such as Joseph, Deborah, Samson, or Peter.

Here are two ways to do a Bible biography:

A. Ask a volunteer each week to write a one-page summary of a Bible person's life. Provide additional biblical references needed for this research. The youth will read the Scriptures and write a brief biography, which he or she will present to the group the following week. This research could be the core of a group study of various personalities of the Bible or lend support to an ongoing study on various themes.

B. Prepare a Bible biography for each weekly class session and select someone to read aloud the biography to the group. Follow up the reading with discussion.

(See example on the next two pages.)

Bible Biography: John the Baptizer

From the beginning, John's life was closely connected to the life and ministry of Jesus of Nazareth. Before John was born, an angel told his mother that she would give birth to a special child, who would be great in the sight of God and who would prepare the people to return to the Lord.

John's father, Zechariah, was a priest in the Temple. But he could scarcely believe the amazing news. He and his wife, Elizabeth, had waited for a child for years; and now they were getting old. Zechariah found that he had lost the power of speech. He would be unable to utter a word until John was born.

Elizabeth had a cousin named Mary, who was also pregnant, with Jesus. When Elizabeth was six months into her pregnancy, Mary came to see her. At the sound of Mary's voice, the baby in Elizabeth's womb leaped for joy; and Elizabeth told Mary, "Blessed are you among women, and blessed is the fruit of your womb."

Finally, when John was born, Zechariah named him; and all of the neighbors were amazed.

When John grew up, he went into the wilderness to proclaim the coming of the kingdom of God. He ate only locusts and wild honey, wore a camel's sash and sandals, and drank no wine. He baptized people in the river Jordan and people came to him, confessing their sin and seeking God.

One day, Jesus came to John to be baptized. John hesitated to baptize Jesus. He had just been telling the other people who came to be baptized, "I am not worthy to untie the thong of his sandals." But after Jesus insisted, John baptized the Lord; and the Holy Spirit descended upon Jesus "in bodily form like a dove."

John told the people, "I baptize you with water; but one who is more powerful than I is coming. . . . He will baptize you with the Holy Spirit and fire."

Later, after John was arrested by Herod and thrown into prison, Jesus called his first disciples and began to teach publicly. Some months later, John the Baptizer was beheaded by Herod. His earthly life ended; but as John had predicted, the powerful ministry of Jesus had just begun.

(Based on Matthew 3:1-17; Mark 1:4-11; 6:14-29; Luke 1:5-80; 3:1-22; John 1:6-34)

4. Sound off

Music obviously has the power to touch the hearts of teenagers. Use music to explore biblical themes and get youth talking about the Bible.

Play popular songs or contemporary Christian music, and invite the teenagers to talk about the lyrics from a biblical perspective. Good questions to ask might include these:

☆ What biblical references did you hear in these lyrics?
☆ Did you notice any biblical principles in this music that could help you in your daily life?
☆ If you were to choose a Bible story to accompany this song, what would it be? Why?
☆ If this song has a theme or focal point, where might you find this same theme in the Bible?

Be aware that many songs can be used to underscore a biblical study or topic and may also be used in a worship segment. Invite the youth to bring in their favorite songs and talk about the biblical themes implied in the lyrics.

5. Hymnal Study

Although hymnals may be falling out of fashion among teenagers, many churches still use them. Many hymns have biblical references sprinkled throughout.

Flip through a hymnal, and you will discover biblical citations printed at the bottom of most hymns. You can begin with a hymn or praise chorus and invite the youth to look up the various Scripture references.

Talk about the Bible stories and ask questions such as these:

☆ Why did the hymn composer or songwriter choose these particular words?
☆ How does the song help us to better understand the biblical story or reference?
☆ What biblical images come to mind when you read the words of this song?

☆ Can you think of other biblical references that are similar, or that could add weight or meaning to this song?

☆ What biblical stories would you use if you were to write a song or hymn? Why?

6. Bible Journal

Journals are big with teenagers, especially girls. Don't overlook the power of providing a Bible journal for your teens to coax them into reading the Bible on a regular basis. A Bible journal can be a simple tool—little more than photocopies stapled together—or a more elaborate tome that you could have printed and bound especially for your group.

One way to create a topnotch journal is to solicit one- or two-sentence faith statements from the teenagers. Put a different quotation on each page along with a selected Bible reading for the day or week. Provide additional space for writing. Presto! You have just created a small journal that teens will enjoy picking up and reading.

Better yet, they can use their journal as a guide to reading the Bible each day or week. Such a journal could also be used as a guide throughout the entire year. It might include Bible lessons or topics that you will be studying in upcoming sessions; or it might focus on a particular book or section of the Bible, perhaps following certain themes or passages the pastor might speak on throughout the year.

As a further way to promote Bible reading, you might include on each page one or two questions based on the Scripture for the day. This way the teens have an opportunity to reflect in private about the Bible lesson they have read.

Consider also using the journals on retreats, outings, or mission trips as a way to cultivate group-building or to establish a focus for a specific task that you hope to accomplish together. A journal can be a fine tool for strengthening a deeper faith and biblical understanding within your youth group.

My Bible Journal

> *"I know God loves me, and I think God loves everyone. But sometimes the hardest part is letting me love someone else."*
>
> —Sylvia (age 16)

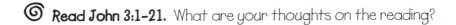 **Read John 3:1-21.** What are your thoughts on the reading?

How do you hope to live in the love of God today?

What kind of love is Jesus talking about?

Prayer for the Day

Dear Lord, may your love shine through me today, so that others will know that you love them. Make me a light and a witness, that others might be drawn to your truth. Amen.

7. The Bible Report

Give the youth a chance to create their own version of a news show or documentary based on a Bible story. The teens will need to work together to read a Bible story, write a script, and report the news they have discovered. This method of teaching the Bible is fun and energizing, and the teenagers will remember the story after they talk about it.

You might use a Bible report or group skit to lead into a discussion of a Bible story. Provide props and costumes for the teens to use for a skit or let them perform a standard newscast while sitting behind a table.

A Bible report can also be a creative way of presenting a Bible story in a worship setting.

8. Bible Timeline

The Bible is a big book and often a difficult one to comprehend. For most teenagers—and adults, for that matter— chronology can be a major obstacle. Who came first, Abraham or Elijah? When did Esther live? How many years fall between the destruction of the first Temple and the birth of Jesus? All these are difficult questions, but important ones if a person is to grasp the general scope and history of the Scriptures.

Help your teenagers grasp chronology by making a Bible timeline of the events and people you are discussing in your study. Never assume that youth know when biblical events took place, or whether Jesus was born after Moses. Help them understand these concepts with the aid of a timeline.

On page 25 is a quick example of a basic timeline (one that you can use as a study guide or game). The answers are below:

Answers to Bible Timeline

2000 B.C. (Abraham)	1000 B.C. (David)	500 B.C. (Nehemiah)	A.D. 70 (Peter's letters)
1200 B.C. (Moses)	700 B.C. (Isaiah)	3 B.C. (Jesus)	A.D. 90 (John's letters)

Bible Timeline

Place the following biblical people and letters on the timeline next to their corresponding dates (✭):

Jesus	Abraham	Isaiah	Nehemiah
Peter's Letters	John's Letters	David	Moses

2000 B.C. 1200 B.C. 1000 B.C. 700 B.C. 500 B.C. 3 B.C. A.D. 70 A.D. 90

9. The Late, Great, Bible Debate

If your youth group enjoys friendly but spirited discussions, you might consider using a form of debate as a study tool. The purpose of such debate, in concept, is to be exposed to various nuances or aspects of biblical understanding or interpretation. Learning how to listen to others—and also how to talk about what we believe—is one of the most maturing and strengthening ways to learn the Scriptures.

You don't have to select hot topics to have a great debate study. Rather, use a pro/con format to help the teenagers tell why they would agree or disagree with a particular position or interpretation.

You may have heard the saying, "We don't really know something until we can explain it to somebody else." Being able to articulate an idea means that learning has truly taken place. The debate format can enable teenagers to hone their skills in expressing their biblical understandings.

Try a debate using these great Bible passages:

✩ **Leviticus 11:1, 7-8** (*prohibition against eating pork*)

—Is this prohibition binding for Christians?

✩ **Psalm 137:8-9** (*prayer for the destruction of children*)

—Is this a prayer that we would ever want to pray?

✩ **Matthew 10:34-39** (*parents against their children*)

—What did Jesus mean by this passage?

✩ **Acts 4:32-35** (*early-church communal living*)

—Should we as the church live out our faith in this manner today?

10. Bible Personalities

One way to help teenagers identify with a Bible narrative is to invite them to imagine themselves being involved in the story. Many Old Testament stories, as well as the parables of Jesus, lend themselves to this style of teaching.

After reading aloud the story, invite the youth to discuss these questions:

☆ Is there someone with whom you can identify in this story? Why?

☆ What actions or feelings in this story are most like your own?

Here are five dramatic Bible stories you can use to help teenagers identify with biblical people:

Genesis 27:1-41 (*Isaac, Rebekah, Jacob, and Esau*)
Genesis 39:7-40:23 (*Joseph, Potiphar's wife, the three prisoners*)
1 Samuel 24:1-22 (*Saul, David, the soldiers*)
Luke 14:16-24 (*parable of the great dinner*)
Luke 15:11-32 (*parable of the prodigal and the elder brother*)

11. Bible Buttons

If your group enjoys discussing hot topics or current affairs, try doing a few Bible buttons. These can be brief readings from the Bible, followed by quick opinions or immediate thoughts. This technique yields a surprising amount of discussion in a brief timespan.

Some good Bible buttons can be found in Proverbs and Matthew.

(See examples on page 28.)

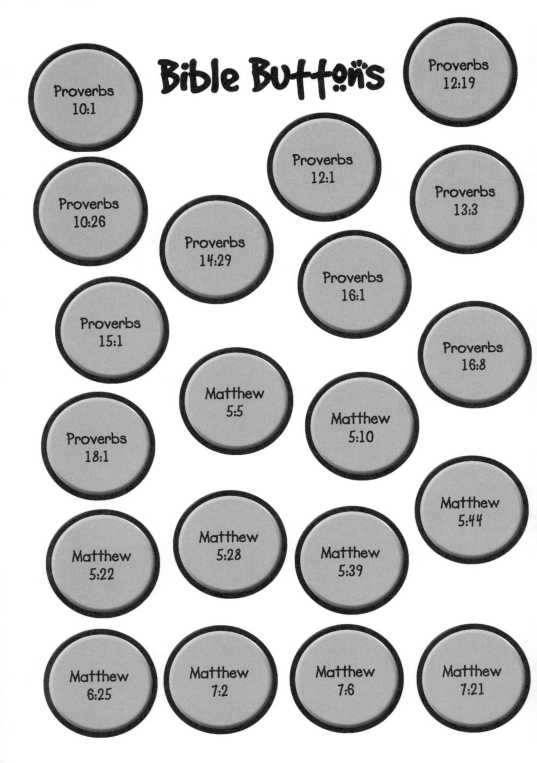

Bible Buttons

Proverbs 10:1

Proverbs 12:19

Proverbs 12:1

Proverbs 10:26

Proverbs 13:3

Proverbs 14:29

Proverbs 16:1

Proverbs 15:1

Proverbs 16:8

Matthew 5:5

Matthew 5:10

Proverbs 18:1

Matthew 5:44

Matthew 5:22

Matthew 5:28

Matthew 5:39

Matthew 6:25

Matthew 7:2

Matthew 7:6

Matthew 7:21

12. Maps & Charts

Think about all of the maps and charts that youth encounter at school—in chemistry, history, geography, English, and statistics, for example. Many teens absorb information much faster by looking at a chart than by simply hearing or reading information in plain text. Use this knowledge to your advantage.

Many Bibles contain maps and charts that are most helpful in understanding the history, culture, and background of ancient times. These items make fantastic visuals or introductions to Bible studies and will also give the youth a bit of geography and sociology to boot.

Most Bible or Christian bookstores will have colorful flip charts as part of their inventory. These resources are well worth the investment and can add much to a Bible study or retreat.

(See the map on page 30.)

13. Worship by Bible

If you have ever wanted an approach to teaching the Bible in a worship setting, consider a worship service created completely from the Bible. You can use this worship at the close of a group meeting, on a retreat, or to establish a worshipful atmosphere at the beginning of a longer study period.

(See "Bible Worship" on page 31.)

ISRAEL IN CANAAN
Joshua to Samuel and Saul

▲ Cities of Refuge
■ Philistine Cities

SCALE OF MILES
0   5   10 15 20 25 30

Sidon

MT. HERMON

Damascus

Dan (Laish)

DAN

Tyre

ASHER

▲ Kadesh

Hazor

BASHAN

ZEBULUN

NAPHTALI

Sea of Chinnereth

Golan

MT. TABOR

ISSACHAR

MANASSEH

▲ Ramoth-gilead

Megiddo

MANASSEH

HILL COUNTRY OF ISRAEL

▲ Shechem

River Jordan

THE ARABAH

GILEAD

MT. GERIZIM

EPHRAIM

GAD

AMMON

Shiloh

Bethel

Ai

Shittim

▲ Bezer

Jericho

MT. PISGAH

BENJAMIN

The Great Sea

DAN

Jerusalem

Ashdod

Ashkelon

PHILISTINES

HILL COUNTRY OF JUDAH

Sea of the Arabah (Salt Sea)

REUBEN

Gaza

JUDAH

Lachish

Hebron
▲

Aroer

River Arnon

Debir

MOAB

Beer-sheba

SIMEON

The Negeb

EDOM

Bible Worship

Call to Worship:
>The LORD is in his holy temple;
>>let all the earth keep silence before him!"
>>>(Habakkuk 2:20)

Hymn (chanted or read to background music):
>Praise the LORD!
>>O give thanks to the LORD, for he is good;
>>for his steadfast love endures forever.
>Who can utter the mighty doings of the LORD,
>>or declare all his praise?
>Happy are those who observe justice,
>>who do righteousness at all times.
>>>(Psalm 106:1-3)

Reading: **Isaiah 40:3-5**

Reading: **Ephesians 5:15-20**

Prayer (in unison): **Philippians 1:3-11**

Gospel Lesson: **Matthew 13:24-30**

Message: **Matthew 13:36b-43**

Response (in unison): **1 Corinthians 9:24-27**

Closing Prayer (or chant):
"I pray that the sharing of your faith may become
effective when you perceive all the good that we may do
for Christ. I have indeed received much joy and
encouragement from your love."

>>>(Philemon 1:6-7)

14. Use a Concordance

If you haven't yet discovered the usefulness of a concordance for studying the Bible, try one out. Many Bibles have a condensed version of a concordance in the back, where it is sometimes called a dictionary.

If your youth group wants to do a study on peace, justice, joy—or on any other subject, for that matter—have them look up a few biblical references for these words and go from there.

While a concordance will not help interpret the Bible, it can lead to various words or phrases contained in the Bible. How often have you wanted to look up a particular verse, but you could recall only one word or phrase in the verse? Or have you ever wanted to cross-reference a word or phrase, but you couldn't recall the location? A concordance can help you find these passages and more.

15. Read the Creed

Many churches recite or confess a creed each Sunday. However, a creed may also be used to explore the biblical basis of the confession.

For a quick and easy creed or Bible study, invite the youth to look up the Bible references in the Apostles' Creed on the following page.

The Apostles' Creed

I believe in God the Father Almighty (1)
   maker of heaven and earth (2);
And in Jesus Christ his only Son our Lord (3):
   who was conceived by the Holy Spirit (4),
      born of the Virgin Mary (5),
      suffered under Pontius Pilate (6),
      was crucified (7), dead, and buried (8);*
   the third day he rose from the dead (9);
   he ascended into heaven (10),
      and sitteth at the right hand of God the Father Almighty (11),
   from thence he shall come to judge the quick and the dead (12).
I believe in the Holy Spirit (13),
   the holy catholic church (14),
   the communion of saints (15),
   the forgiveness of sins (16),
   the resurrection of the body (17),
   and the life everlasting (18). Amen.

Other versions include "He descended into hell (19)."

(1) Genesis 1:1; Philippians 1:2, and so forth
(2) Genesis 1:1
(3) John 1:18
(4) Luke 1:31; Matthew 1:18
(5) Luke 1:34; 2:7
(6) Mark 15:15
(7) Luke 23:33
(8) Luke 23:46; John 19:40-42
(9) Luke 24:1-2
(10) Acts 1:9
(11) Mark 14:62
(12) Matthew 13:41-43
(13) Acts 1:5; 1 John 3:24
(14) Matthew 16:18; 1 Corinthians 12:12
(15) Hebrews 10:24-25; 12:1
(16) 1 John 1:8-9
(17) 1 Corinthians 15:35-44
(18) 1Thessalonians 4:17; 1 Peter 1:3-4
(19) 1 Peter 3:19-20

16. Short Stuff

A Bible lesson doesn't have to be lengthy to be effective; and we don't have to read lengthy passages in order to gain some measure of understanding of the Bible. How about a study using some of the shortest books of the Bible? Most of the short books can be read in only a few minutes; and with a bit of discussion, you can knock out a topnotch study in less than half an hour.

Have the youth read a few of these books in their totality or divide them in half if time is short:

Ruth	**2 Peter**	**Jonah**	**2 John**
Haggai	**3 John**	**Titus**	**Jude**
Philemon			

17. Bible Brainstorm

Not all Bible studies have to be structured to be successful or helpful. For a little diversity, give a Bible brainstorm a try.

Gather the youth into a circle, distribute Bibles, and allow each person to choose a passage that he or she wants to read to the group. This doesn't necessarily have to be a favorite text; it could even be selected by simply opening the Bible and flipping through a few pages.

After each Bible passage is read aloud, invite responses or thoughts or have a time of silent prayer.

18. Parable Charades

The parables of Jesus are some of the more memorable stories of the Bible. Not only are they rich with meaning, but the parables also provide excellent opportunities for teenagers to recall details of the story through action and retelling.

So if you would like to introduce a bit of movement into your Bible teaching, try Bible charades. First, make a list of several action-packed parables. If you'd like, provide a few props for the charades, such as various hats and other simple articles of clothing. Then invite the youth to divide into teams of three or four. Give each team a parable, which they must act out in front of the other groups. The other groups guess what parable is being portrayed.

Following each group's parable charade, read the parable aloud from the Bible. Use these questions for discussion:

⭐ What new insights did you receive from seeing the parable acted out as well as read?

⭐ What is the meaning of this parable?

⭐ What does this parable tell us about God? about people?

⭐ What elements of the story give this parable its power?

Good parables to use for Bible charades include but are not limited to the following:

Matthew 13:1-9 *(the parable of the seeds)*
Matthew 21:33-39 *(the parable of the vineyard)*
Luke 10:30-37 *(the parable of the good Samaritan)*
Luke 15:3-7 *(the parable of the lost sheep)*
Luke 15:8-10 *(the parable of the lost coin)*
Luke 15:11-32 *(the parable of the lost son)*

19. Hot Topics

Your group may already have in mind a few hot topics that produce stimulating conversation. If not, invite the teenagers to write on index cards a few topics that they would like to discuss or study. Evaluate the topics within the group and decide which ones are most worthy of conversation.

Use a concordance or Bible dictionary to locate biblical references that may aid in a study of the topic. Divide these references among the group, and invite the teens to read these passages aloud. Follow up with discussion.

If you want to conduct a hot-topics study, set a few guidelines to aid the discussion. I have found these guidelines to be most helpful with youth:

1. Respect others' opinions. Listen to what others have to say in entirety before offering your opinion.

2. Be aware that others may disagree with your opinions or interpretation.

3. When possible, seek understanding or, perhaps, a middle ground.

4. Pray for one another.

5. Let love and unity prevail.

20. Experiencing the Psalms

Adolescence is an emotional period of life. In fact, most teenagers have strong feelings about a great many things. Sometimes, these emotions can be used quite effectively in a Bible study.

Reading the Psalms is one way to help youth explore their feelings and find comfort and challenge in the Scriptures. These prayers and poems of the Bible are excellent devotional material and provide the words many teenagers long to say to God and others.

By choosing a half dozen psalms and reading them to your group, you can offer a study that can open up many feelings among your teenagers. Read the passages, then ask a few of these questions to get at the heart of their spirit:

☆ What feelings were evoked by this psalm?

☆ Can you think of a time in your life when you felt the way the psalmist apparently did?

☆ What phrases can you recall from the psalm that are meaningful to you?

☆ What emotions are being expressed to God in this psalm?

☆ What attitudes are evident in this psalm?

☆ What might this psalm teach us about how to live?

☆ Are there areas in your life where you need to apply the words of this psalm?

☆ How would you express in your own words what this psalm is saying?

21. Heroes and Villains

One unique angle from which to study the Bible involves taking a look at the heroes and villains of old. Teenagers enjoy the drama this Bible perspective offers and can identify with those who overcame with God's help.

Some of the most interesting Bible pairs include the following:

> **Moses and Pharaoh** (*Exodus 5:1–6:1*)
>
> **Deborah and Sisera** (*Judges 4*)
>
> **Samson and the Philistines** (*Judges 16:21-30*)
>
> **David and Goliath** (*1 Samuel 17*)
>
> **Esther and Haman** (*Esther 9:1-17*)
>
> **Jesus and Pilate** (*John 19:1-20:9*)

22. Bible Interview

Wouldn't it be wonderful if we could open the Bible and read an actual interview involving God and a particular person, or between two persons? Well, why not give it a try? Here's how:

With a bit of ingenuity and practice, you can create an interview composed entirely of biblical dialogue. Use a Bible interview as a devotion or a skit. Follow up with discussion or opinions.

(See "Bible Interview With Jonah," on pages 39–40.)

Bible Interview With Jonah

GOD: Go at once to Nineveh, that great city, and cry out against it; for their wickedness has come up before me.

NARRATOR: But Jonah set out to flee to Tarshish from the presence of the LORD. He went down to Joppa and found a ship going to Tarshish; so he paid his fare and went on board. . . . But the LORD hurled a great wind upon the sea. . . . So the [sailors] picked Jonah up and threw him into the sea. . . . But the LORD provided a large fish to swallow up Jonah.

JONAH: I called to the LORD out of my distress, and he answered me; out of the belly of Sheol I cried, and you heard my voice.

NARRATOR: Then the LORD spoke to the fish, and it spewed Jonah out upon the dry land.

GOD: Get up, [Jonah], go to Nineveh, that great city, and proclaim to it the message that I tell you.

NARRATOR: Jonah began to go into the city, going a day's walk. And he cried out.

JONAH: Forty days more, and Nineveh shall be overthrown!

NARRATOR: The people of Nineveh believed God; they proclaimed a fast, and everyone, great and small, put on sackcloth. . . . When God saw what they did, how they turned from their evil ways, God changed his mind about the calamity that he had said he would bring upon them; and he did not do it.

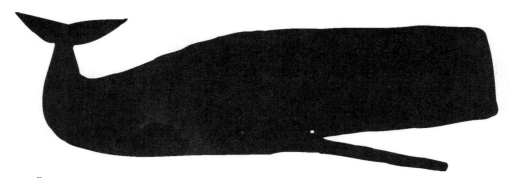

JONAH: O LORD! Is not this what I said while I was still in my own country? That is why I fled to Tarshish at the beginning; for I knew that you are a gracious God and merciful, slow to anger, and abounding in steadfast love, and ready to relent from punishing. And now, O LORD, please take my life from me, for it is better for me to die than to live.

GOD: Is it right for you to be angry?

NARRATOR: God appointed a bush. . . . to give shade over [Jonah's] head. . . . But when dawn came up the next day, God appointed a worm that attacked the bush, so that it withered.

JONAH: It is better for me to die than to live.

GOD: Is it right for you to be angry about the bush?

JONAH: Yes, angry enough to die.

GOD: You are concerned about the bush, for which you did not labor and which you did not grow; it came into being in a night and perished in a night. And should I not be concerned about Nineveh . . . in which there are more than a hundred and twenty thousand persons who do not know their right hand from their left?

23. Bible Speed Read

Here's a teaching technique that is not only quick but also effective in producing verbal responses from teenagers. You can use this idea for those times when you have only a few minutes left in a meeting or if you have a group of teenagers who are not very talkative.

Gather everyone into a circle and invite one of the teens to read aloud a passage from the Bible. Follow up with these questions:

⭐ What images or thoughts came to mind as you heard this passage of the Bible?

⭐ Which words in this Bible passage were particularly helpful ones?

⭐ Which words in this Bible passage were difficult to understand?

⭐ Can you summarize this Bible passage in your own words?

24. The Bible Behind the Symbols

Most church buildings are filled with symbols, both ancient and modern, that point us to biblical stories and lessons. Use symbolism to help the youth visualize biblical aspects of the faith.

As a starting point, here are several symbols and some selected Bible references that can help you teach from these visuals:

John 6:48; Matthew 25:26

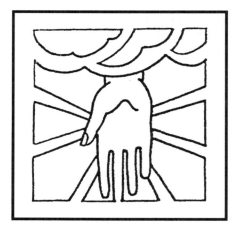

Psalm 102:25

Genesis 1:31

Psalm 33:18

Revelation 2:10

Psalm 119:105

John 19:2

John 11:25

Matthew 16:18

Romans 12:5

Matthew 28:19

Luke 3:22

Acts 2:14; Revelation 5:12

Matthew 28:19

John 1:29

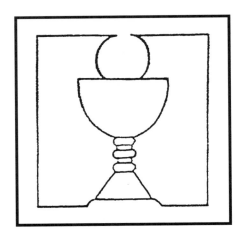

Luke 22:14-20

Show Me the Way

PART TWO

Bible Learning Games

Bible learning doesn't have to be boring. In fact, you can teach the Bible effectively through the use of games, humor, and just plain fun.

Keep in mind that a Bible learning game can be used as a discussion starter or as the center of a learning time. Many of these games would also be appropriate for groups of all ages—including parent/teen nights. Teenagers will be more energetic about gleaning truths from the Bible and remember them longer if you make learning a fun activity.

Show Me the Way

25. Who Said It?

If quotations are your bag or if you'd like to give youth a handle for remembering who in the Bible said what, play this simple, fast-paced game with the youth. Collect a few of your favorite quotations from the Bible, gather the teenagers into a circle (or play by teams), read a quotation, and challenge the teens to identify who said it. Assign a point value to each quotation. Discuss the quotations after each successful guess, and ask the teenagers what the quotation means.

This game is a fantastic way to get your teenagers talking (or guessing); and if your group plays it often enough, they are bound to get a firmer knowledge of who in the Bible said what.

To get you started, here are a dozen quotations and their attributions to use in your first game:

⭐ "I did not laugh."—Sarah (Genesis 18:15)

⭐ "Let my people go."—Moses & Aaron while quoting the Lord (Exodus 5:1)

⭐ "The LORD gave, and the LORD has taken away."—Job (Job 1:21)

⭐ "Truly I do not know how to speak, for I am only a boy."—Jeremiah (Jeremiah 1:6)

⭐ "I baptize you with water for repentance, but one who is more powerful than I is coming after me."—John the Baptizer (Matthew 3:11)

⭐ "Blessed are the peacemakers."—Jesus (Matthew 5:9)

⭐ "You are the light of the world."—Jesus (Matthew 5:14)

⭐ "Lord, if another member of the church sins against me, how often should I forgive? As many as seven times?"—Peter (Matthew 18:21)

⭐ "Truly I tell you, one of you will betray me."—Jesus (Matthew 26:21)

⭐ "Whom do you want me to release for you, Jesus Barabbas or Jesus who is called the Messiah?"—Pontius Pilate (Matthew 27:17)

⭐ "Here am I, the servant of the Lord."—Mary, mother of Jesus (Luke 1:38)

⭐ "Athenians, I see how extremely religious you are in every way."—Paul (Acts 17:22)

26. The Name Game

Before your meeting, prepare self-adhesive nametags. Write the names of Bible people (men and women) on the tags. Put at least one Bible name on each tag.

The purpose of this game is for each participant to learn something about a Bible person and then introduce himself or herself to the rest of the group as that person. When you are ready to play the game, give each youth a name tag and a Bible. Each person will have ten to fifteen minutes to find out as much as possible about his or her Bible person.

For example, a teenager who receives a tag with the name "Noah" might read selected passages from Genesis (6:9-19; 7:1-10; 8:6-22) and use these passages to create an introduction.

Teenagers will not only find this game entertaining, they will also learn much about various people of the Bible. Be prepared to help the youth find the appropriate Bible passages for their information. You may use the Bible People guide below as a starting point.

Bible People

Abraham (Genesis 18:1-15; 25:7)
Sarah (Genesis 18:1-15; 21:1-8; 23:1)
Deborah (Judges 4:1-22)
Samson (Judges 13:2-7; 15:14-17; 16:28-30)
Ruth (Ruth 1:1-5, 15-18; 4:13-17)
Hannah (1 Samuel 1:3-28)
Samuel (1 Samuel 3:1-19)
Job (Job 1:1-22)
John the Baptizer (Mark 1:1-8; Luke 3:1-9)
Simon Peter (Luke 5:1-11; 22:54-62)

27. Bible Trivia

Many Bible trivia games are on the market. These games can be used to teach simple facts about the Bible, including historical facts about people and events. Playing the game on a regular schedule can help teens learn both basic and advanced facts about the Scriptures.

However, if you don't have a Bible trivia game on hand, you can create you own trivia game easily; and you can involve the youth at the same time. Here's how:

Begin by giving each teen five to ten index cards, a pencil, and a Bible. Challenge each teenager to create several trivia questions by perusing the Bible. Have them write on one side of the card the question and the Scripture reference. The teens may label each question as "difficult," "moderate," or "easy." Then ask them to be sure to write on the back of the card the correct answer. Collect the cards when the teens have finished.

To play, divide the group into teams; or for a less competitive event, have the youth ask a partner the questions. Play for fun, or award points and keep score by teams.

Bonus Idea: Have three colors of index cards for the different categories: "difficult," "moderate," or "easy." Or use cards of different colors for "people," "places," or "events."

Don't throw away the cards after you have used them. Store them in a file box. Each time you play the game, add new cards to the file; and soon you will have a sizable collection of trivia cards, which you can use as time fillers or to take on retreats. Bible trivia questions make a fantastic way to pass the time when your youth group is traveling on a bus or van.

28. Word Games

This game is a fast way to teach teenagers how to use a concordance or other Bible reference work.

First, consider the biblical words that sound theological or strange to teenagers. Words such as *sacrifice, grace, calling, atonement, parable,* or *justification* are just some of the many terms that may elude teenagers (and adults, for that matter). Make a list of words, which might also include people and places; and assign one or two words to each teen.

Show the teenagers how to look up the various words in a concordance to find the corresponding Scripture passages. Have the teens write down the passages and then tell the rest of the group what they have learned about their words.

A Bible dictionary might also be a useful resource. But be ready to offer help or insights as needed.

To make a game of this, compile a list of words that you want the teenagers to find. Divide the group into teams, and divide the words among them. Then heat things up by giving the teams a set amount of time to find out what their words mean and, perhaps, also to tell the biblical passages associated with each word.

When the time is up, each team will report the information about their words. Discuss the various meanings and nuances of the terms.

Use some of the following words as a starting place the first time you play:

Covenant	Eternal Life	Faith
Forgiveness	Grace	Holy Spirit
Hypocrisy	Justice	Lord
Messiah	Sin	Wholeness
Worship	Yahweh	

29. Bible Top Ten

This game is a fantastic way to make your teenagers think about what they believe and why. You can use the Bible as a guide to create a game that will provoke deep, heartfelt discussions about any biblical topic. Here's how it works:

Use a large marker to label ten sheets of paper with a number from *1* to *10*—one number per sheet. Tape the papers to the floor, with the paper labeled *1* in one corner of the room and the paper labeled *10* in the opposite corner. Tape the other sheets in order in between. Leave plenty of space between the numbers so that there will be room for the youth to stand or move about without disturbing the papers.

Then make a list of Bible statements you want the youth to think about. Some of these might be simple; others more difficult.

To play: Tell the participants that when you read aloud a statement, they are to stand next to the number that corresponds most closely to their level of certainty or commitment. Let *10* represent "absolute certainty" and *1* represent "very doubtful." The other numbers will represent various levels of doubt or certainty between *1* and *10*. Each time you read a statement, each person may change his or her position, depending on how he or she feels about that statement.

Read the statements slowly to allow time for the teenagers to commit. Take note of the statements that provoke the most doubt or certainty within the group. Follow up with discussion or a lesson on any or all of those topics.

If you are pressed for time, here are some examples of Bible statements to get you started:

A. God created the heavens and the earth.

B. The Bible contains 66 books.

C. Moses killed a man.

D. David's middle name was Goliath.

E. Jesus was a miracle worker.

F. Jesus never got angry.

G. The Bible says that everyone has sinned.

H. Jesus never sinned.

I. The Bible tells us what to wear.

J. The Bible tells us how the world will end.

30. Bible Bingo

Here's a wonderful mixer that will get your teenagers talking and thinking at the same time.

Before the meeting, prepare a Bingo grid (without the B-I-N-G-O at the top), which contains five rows of five squares. Write a simple fact from the Bible in each square. Be sure to leave a bit of extra space in each square for writing.

As the youth arrive, give each one a Bible Bingo sheet; and invite the teenagers to begin milling around to find people who know the answers to questions in the various squares on the Bingo grid. When a teen locates someone who knows the answer for a particular square, he or she asks that person to sign his or her name inside that square. (If the group is large, you might impose a rule that a teen may not sign his or her own sheet and that no one may sign the same sheet twice.)

Plan to give a small prize to the first teen to have five squares in a row signed. If there is more time, give the prize to the first teen to fill in his or her Bible Bingo sheet with signatures.

See page 56 for a sample Bible Bingo sheet.

THROWN TO THE LIONS	FISHERMEN BROTHERS	NUMBER OF GOSPELS	NUMBER OF PSALMS	WISE KING OF ISRAEL
SIGNATURE	SIGNATURE	SIGNATURE	SIGNATURE	SIGNATURE
HE BECAME PAUL	SUCCESSOR TO MOSES	PLACE OF SACRIFICE	PROPHET TAKEN UP IN A CHARIOT	MOTHER OF JESUS
SIGNATURE	SIGNATURE	SIGNATURE	SIGNATURE	SIGNATURE
WRESTLED WITH AN ANGEL	BUILT THE ARK	Free Space	FIRST BOOK IN THE BIBLE	OLDEST MAN IN THE BIBLE
SIGNATURE	SIGNATURE		SIGNATURE	SIGNATURE
LED ISRAELITES THROUGH RED SEA	LAST BOOK IN THE BIBLE	GIANT SLAIN BY DAVID	FIRST COMMAND-MENT	BAPTIZED JESUS
SIGNATURE	SIGNATURE	SIGNATURE	SIGNATURE	SIGNATURE
PLACE OF JESUS' BIRTH	ABRAHAM'S WIFE	HE BETRAYED JESUS	EVE'S HUSBAND	KING OF EGYPT
SIGNATURE	SIGNATURE	SIGNATURE	SIGNATURE	SIGNATURE

31. Word Find & Crossword Puzzles

A plethora of Bible crossword puzzle books, word finds, and word search puzzles are on the market. And several computer programs are also available that will allow the aspiring youth leader to create his or her own puzzles.

Puzzles can be used to spark interest in a Bible topic or story and can provide some of the key words or concepts that can help you with a discussion. Below is one example of a Bible Word Search that you can use in your next meeting.

Bonus Idea: Many teenagers love to create puzzles. Don't overlook the possibility of inviting a few of your aspiring puzzle makers to create word searches or crosswords for your group to use.

Word Search Answers *(See page 58.)*

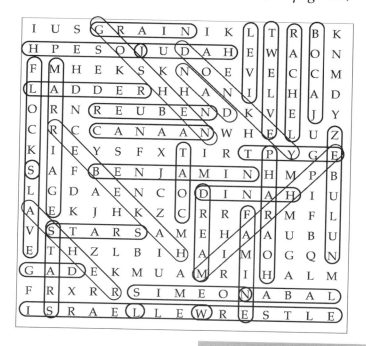

Word Search

```
I U S G R A I N I K L T R B K
H P E S O J U D A H E W A O N
F M H E K S K N O E V E C C M
L A D D E R H H A N I L H A D
O R N R E U B E N D K V E J Y
C R C C A N A A N W H E L U Z
K I E Y S F X T I R T P Y G E
S A F B E N J A M I N H M P B
L G D A E N C O D I N A H I U
A E K J H K Z C R R F R M F L
V S T A R S A M E H A A U B U
E T H Z L B I H A I M O G Q N
G A D E K M U A M R I H A L M
F R X R R S I M E O N A B A L
I S R A E L L E W R E S T L E
```

Word List

ASHER
BENJAMIN
CANAAN
COAT
DAN
DINAH
DONKEY
DREAM
EGYPT
EPHRAIM

FAMINE
FLOCKS
GAD
GOSHEN
GRAIN
ISRAEL
JACOB
JOSEPH
JUDAH
LABAN
LADDER
LEVI

MARRIAGE
PHARAOH
RACHEL
REBEKAH
REUBEN
SIMEON
SLAVE
STARS (appears twice)
TWELVE
WELL
WRESTLE
ZEBULUN

32. Bible Quizzes

A quiz might not seem like a welcome item in a youth group, but it all depends upon how you present it (look at the success of TV quiz shows through the years). I've used quizzes for years with teenagers and have created many fun and inspiring lessons in a test-like format. Don't forget that teenagers are used to taking tests.

But a Bible quiz in a youth group can be non-competitive and helpful. The goal is not a grade, but fun learning. Toss in a few crazy questions, and you've got a quiz your teenagers will want to take again.

"The Jesus Quiz," beginning on page 60, is an example of a quiz that teens would love to take.

Answer Key to The Jesus Quiz

1. c (Luke 2:5-7)
2. b (Luke 2:46)
3. b (Luke 3:23)
4. a (Mark 1:9)
5. b (Luke 4:1-2)
6. a (Hebrews 4:15)
7. d (Mark 8:29)
8. b (John 15:12-15)
9. b (John 11:43-44; Mark 5:39-41)
10. b (The New Testament didn't exist until later.)
11. a (Mark 6:48-49)
12. b (Matthew 19:21)
13. c (John 18:5)
14. d (Luke 8:25)
15. d (Matthew 25:13, 37-46; Mark 13:32)
16. a (John 12:15)
17. a (Mark 14:15)
18. f (Mark 14:37; John 18:10; Mark 14:45)
19. c (Luke 23:6-7)
20. c (Mark 15:15)
21. a (Mark 15:26)
22. b (Mark 14:50)
23. b (Luke 23:32)
24. c (Luke 24:1-3)
25. b (Luke 24:30-31)

The Jesus Quiz

Circle the answer that you believe comes closest to what the Bible tells us about Jesus. If you don't know the answer, don't ask a friend. However, if you'd like to, you may flip a coin or roll on the floor in a tantrum.

1. Jesus' mother was _____.

a. Martha Stewart

b. a good sport

c. Mary

d. Eve

2. What was Jesus doing in the Temple when he was twelve?

a. writing on the walls

b. talking to the elder

c. driving away money changers

d. sleeping

3. How old was Jesus when he began to teach publicly?

a. not old enough

b. about thirty

c. twelve

d. over the hill

4. Who baptized Jesus?

a. John

b. Peter

c. a priest

d. his father

5. True or False: Jesus was never tempted to sin.

a. True

b. False

6. True or False: Jesus never sinned.

a. True

b. False

7. Who was the first disciple to make a public confession of Jesus as Messiah?

a. Judas
b. the Grand Inquisitor

c. Mary Magdalene
d. Peter

8. True or False: Jesus never thought of his disciples as friends.

a. True

b. False

9. Whom did Jesus raise from the dead?

a. King David
b. Lazarus and a little girl

c. Lazarus
d. the witch of Endor

10. True or False: When Jesus taught, he always read from the New Testament.

a. True

b. False

11. Jesus once walked on what body of water?

a. the Sea of Galilee
b. the Mediterranean Sea

c. the Nile
d. the Atlantic Ocean

12. Jesus once asked a rich young ruler to give _____ to the poor.

a. a decent haircut
b. his wealth

c. love
d. a round of applause

13. Which of Jesus' disciples betrayed him?

a. Doubting Thomas
b. Earl the sandal-maker

c. Judas Iscariot
d. Mad Max

14. After Jesus calmed a storm, what question did his disciples ask?

a. "When is it going to snow?"
b. "Will you now restore the kingdom to Israel?"
c. "Got Milk?"
d. "Who is this, that even the wind and water obey him?"

15. What did Jesus teach his followers about the end of time?

a. Watch and be prepared.

b. Blessed are those who are working for the Kingdom when the end comes.

c. No one knows when the end will be—not even Jesus—only the Father.

d. All of the above

16. Jesus rode into Jerusalem a final time on _____ .

a. a donkey or colt

b. an elephant

c. a white horse

d. a flying carpet

17. Where did Jesus celebrate a final Passover meal with his disciples?

a. in a furnished upper room

b. at a nice restaurant

c. at the home of Mary and Martha

d. in the Temple

18. Which of the following happened in Gethsemane, on the Mount of Olives?

a. The disciples fell asleep while Jesus prayed.

b. Peter denied that he knew Jesus.

c. Peter cut off a servant's ear.

d. Judas betrayed Jesus with a kiss.

e. all of the above.

f. a, c, & d

19. Jesus appeared before which ruler(s)?

a. Herod

b. Pontius Pilate

c. a & b

d. Caesar Augustus & Agrippa

20. What was the name of the prisoner who was released instead of Jesus?

a. Barnabas

b. Barnaby

c. Barabbas

d. Bartholomew

21. For what crime was Jesus condemned to death?

a. treason against Rome—calling himself a king

b. for making a mess of the Temple

c. for speaking out against the religious authorities

d. for being of the wrong political party

22. True or False: The disciples stayed to watch Jesus die on the cross.

a. True

b. False

23. True or False: Jesus was the only person to die by crucifixion.

a. True

b. False

24. The first people to witness the empty tomb were _____.

a. Doubting Thomas and James

b. James and John

c. the women

d. the Roman soldiers

25. When/how did the disciples of Emmaus recognize Jesus after his resurrection?

a. when Jesus revealed his nail-scarred hands

b. when Jesus broke the bread

c. when Jesus told them a parable

d. all of the above

26. I think that Jesus is_____.

a. cool

b. Lord

c. Savior

d. All of the above

33. Who Am I?

This game is great for teaching youth about people in the Bible. Your teenagers will learn about biblical people in a step-by-step format.

Prepare for the game by making a list of several Bible persons and five facts for each person. Rate the facts, in order, from the most difficult fact, 5, to the easiest, 1. Points are awarded according to the rating.

Ask the youth, "Who am I?" Then read aloud the most difficult fact. If, after the first fact is read, someone guesses who the Bible person is, he or she gets 5 points. If someone guesses who the Bible person is after you've read the second most difficult fact, he or she receives 4 points. As more facts are read, the points earned decrease accordingly. The person with the highest score after the round is the champion.

Use this game to lead into a discussion about a particular personality or Bible event. Or play the game for fun. Here are some examples:

1. Who Am I?

5. I am an Israelite.
4. I am a priest.
3. I was taken into captivity in Babylon.
2. I have had many visions of God's glory.
1. I saw a wheel turning in the sky.

2. Who Am I?

5. I am a woman.
4. You might say that I am an original.
3. I know a talking snake.
2. I ate forbidden fruit.
1. My husband is Adam.

3. Who Am I?

5. I live in Capernaum of Galilee.
4. Jesus healed my mother-in-law.
3. My brother is Andrew.
2. I am a fisherman.
1. I denied that I knew Jesus.

4. Who Am I?

5. A book of the Bible is named after me.
4. I am a follower of Jesus.
3. I am one of the Twelve.
2. I collected taxes.
1. Jesus called me in my tax office to become a disciple.

5. Who Am I?

5. I am a woman.
4. I married a king.
3. I am a hero.
2. I saved my people.
1. I saved my people from an evil man named Haman.

Answers: 1. *Ezekiel the prophet,* 2. *Eve,* 3. *Peter,* 4. *Matthew,* 5. *Esther*

34. Who Wants to be a Disciple?

If you are looking for a game show format to be used at that next large youth gathering, try this one. All you'll need are some serious-looking teenage contestants and a set of questions and answers about discipleship. Assign points or small prizes to the questions. Ask questions of increasing difficulty and value as the game goes along. Have the youth play individually or as teams.

See page 67 for a sample list of questions.

Who Wants to Be a Disciple?

for fun

Which of the following did Jesus say his disciples would receive?

a. forgiveness, love, peace, persecution, eternal life
b. smooth sailing
c. money, sex, and power
d. long life, good health

(Answer: a)

for one penny

How many disciples did Jesus originally call?

a. 9
b. a bunch

c. just a few
d. 12

(Answer: d)

for a nickel

A disciple is someone who _____.

a. wears a WWJD wristband
b. goes to church a lot

c. makes lots of noise
d. learns from a teacher

(Answer: d)

for a Kiddie Meal

Complete this quotation by Jesus: "All people will know you are my disciples if _____."

a. you drive a nice car
b. you wear a WWJD wristband

c. you listen to Christian music
d. you love one another

(Answer: d)

for All the Marbles

What was the last commandment Jesus gave his disciples?

a. "Get the parking space closest to the church door."
b. "Make WWJD bracelets."
c. "Go into all the world and proclaim the good news.
d. "Play that funky music.

(Answer: c)

35. Bible Scavenger Hunt

Here is a fun, Bible-learning game that will get your teenagers moving. You'll need several Bibles, several rooms, and a scavenger hunt list.

This scavenger hunt is played in the usual manner; but instead of looking for an item, teens will be looking for clues in the Bible. I've played this game many times with teens, and they truly enjoy the challenge that the game provides. Here's how it works:

Before the meeting, prepare a scavenger hunt list (or photocopy the Bible Hunt Clues, on page 69). Arrange several Bibles in several rooms. Open each Bible to the appropriate page, and place a bookmark in it in case the Bible is closed by accident. If you have twenty clues, you will need twenty Bibles, opened to the page containing the answer. The youth will go from room to room to find the answers to the various clues. If you have a small group, the Bibles can be arranged on tables around one room.

The first person or team to complete the list wins. Or set a time limit for the game, and see which person or team gets the most answers within the time limit.

After the game, discuss the answers to dig deeper into the stories behind the clues.

Answer Key *(For the Leader)*

1. Stars, sun, moon (Genesis 1:14-19)
2. Noah (Genesis 6:19)
3. Gomer (Hosea 1:3)
4. Lamentations
5. Song of Solomon
6. Job
7. Ass/Donkey (Judges 15:16)
8. The Woman of Samaria (John 4:16-18)
9. Magi/wise men (Matthew 2:1-12)
10. Simon & Andrew (Matthew 5:18-20)
11. Naaman (2 Kings 4:8-14)
12. As you would have them do to you (Matthew 7:12)
13. Treasure (Matthew 13:44)
14. Angel (Matthew 28:2)
15. Acts
16. Romans
17. Paul, shipwrecked on Malta Island (Acts 27:43–28:1)
18. Jude
19. Martha (Luke 10:38-41)
20. Amen (Revelation 22:21)

Show Me the Way

Bible Hunt Clues

1. On the fourth day of Creation, these were made.
2. This old man, he played two by two.
3. His wife wasn't in the Marines, but she may have been a Pyle.
4. Ah, this book of the Bible is to weep.
5. He had a lot to sing about, so he wrote his own song.
6. He never lost his "job," but he sure did suffer.
7. The jawbone of a what?
8. Men just loved her.
9. Not Larry, Moe, and Curly, but wise guys nonetheless.
10. First followers.
11. When you gotta go, you gotta go. And he went seven times.
12. Do what to others?
13. It may be the kingdom of heaven, but some people bury it.
14. A whole lot of shakin' was goin' on when this dude showed up.
15. This book sounds a lot like "Ax."
16. Friends, these dudes, and countrymen, lend me your ears.
17. I wonder if he knew Gilligan?
18. Didn't the Beatles sing this one?
19. I hear she was a good cook, too.
20. It's always the last word.

Show Me the Way

PART THREE

Ready-to-Go Retreats & Bible Studies

Opportunities for Bible learning can be found at any time, so be ready to take advantage of these moments. Retreats are excellent for delving deeper into the Bible or for focusing on a topic or theme. Mission trips and service projects can also provide opportunities for Bible reflection and meditation. And meaningful Bible studies can be planned for camp outs, summer camps, and conferences.

Youth are, perhaps, most open to Bible study when they are facing great challenges or when a special mission or event requires deeper devotion and reflection. Many teenagers lack the focus or self-discipline to study the Bible on their own; but they are eager to read and study with a group, especially when a special time or mood has been established.

Take advantage of these times by preparing a Bible study that is right for your group. In this part, you will find ready-to-go Bible study ideas for your next special event or outing.

Show Me the Way

36. Mission-Trip Marvels

(A mission-trip study of the apostle Paul's journeys)

This study will provide an overview of Paul's missionary journeys and his correspondence with the churches he helped establish during his travels. As the youth examine Paul's life and teachings, they will be challenged to become disciples and serve others. Conduct the study in three separate sessions, or use it in a retreat setting as preparation for a mission trip or as background for a service project.

For this study you will need Bibles, paper, and pencils.

Part 1: Paul's Early Travels

Gather the youth into a circle and invite them to summarize Paul's early life. Ask:

⭐ What was Paul like before he was a Christian? (Acts 8:1; 9:1-9)
⭐ What events led up to Paul's conversion?
⭐ What changes took place in Paul? (Acts 9:10-22)
⭐ How did the disciples react to Paul's changed life?
⭐ How would you summarize the early Christian mission?

Read Acts 13:13-52 *(in groups or aloud).*

Distribute paper and pencils and ask the youth to list the various places that Paul visited, what happened in those places, and the responses of the people there.

Then ask:

⭐ What was Paul's message to the people of these towns?
⭐ How is this message helpful for us today?
⭐ How is it helpful to us in our mission or service?

Ask the youth to list the challenges that they believe they will face in their mission. Have the youth talk in small groups about some of these challenges and how faith and working together can alleviate fear and doubts about the service.

Part 2: Paul's Further Journeys

Read Acts 17 & Acts 18:1-4 *(in groups or aloud).*

Distribute paper and pencils, and ask the youth to list the various places Paul visited. Then have the youth list the people who were with Paul on these journeys and any reactions from the people in the different towns. Then ask:

☆ Why, do you think, was it important for Paul to have another believer with him on his journey?

☆ What were some reactions of the people in the various towns?

☆ Why, do you think, did Paul have success establishing a church in Thessalonica but difficulty in Athens?

☆ In what ways did Paul change his message or method in each of the various towns? Why was that so?

Then have the youth form two teams. Have one team read **1 Thessalonians 4:1-12** and the other team read **1 Corinthians 3**. Then invite each team to tell their responses to these questions:

☆ What concerns did Paul communicate to the people of this church in his letter?

☆ What attitudes or problems are mentioned?

☆ How are these churches different? similar?

☆ How might Paul's advice to the early churches help us in our mission?

☆ What insights can you find that can help us in our service to others?

Part 3: Paul's Last Journeys

Read Acts 19 (*in groups or aloud*).

   Distribute paper and pencils and ask the youth to list the names of churches Paul visited, who was with him, and the responses of the people. Then ask:

★ What events shaped these journeys of Paul's?
★ Who accompanied Paul on these trips?
★ Who caused trouble for the mission? How?

   Then have the youth form two teams. Ask one team to read **Ephesians 1** and the other team to read **Galatians 1**. Then ask:

★ What important matters was Paul trying to convey to these churches?
★ What challenges did these churches face?
★ What important matters should we keep before us as we go on this mission?
★ If Paul were to write our group a letter, what might he say to us?
★ How might we best live out our discipleship on this mission trip?

37. Meeting Places

(A study for an evening camp out)

A Bible study around the campfire can be a perfect opportunity to encounter God. So why not talk about some sacred places mentioned in the Bible?

This study can be conducted in a single session or completed at different intervals. If you have a large group, consider dividing the youth into small groups or have them work with partners. Only Bibles will be needed for this outdoor study.

The Oaks of Mamre

Begin the session with these three questions:

★ Can you think of a place where you have experienced the presence of God?
★ Why, do you think, have human beings always marked certain spaces as holy or set apart for God?
★ What makes a place special to us?

Read Genesis 18:1-15 *(in groups or aloud)*. Then ask:

★ Why, do you think, was Abraham sitting near the oaks?
★ What event or announcement took place near the oaks of Mamre?
★ How did Abraham react to this announcement? How did Sarah react?
★ How did Abraham and Sarah experience the presence of God in this place?
★ What did Abraham do to make the place memorable or special?

The House of God

Begin the session by asking these questions:

★ What makes a place a "house of God"?

★ Can you think of times in your life when you have experienced God's presence in a place set aside for worship? If so, what happened?

★ What are some ways we might mark a holy place today?

Read Genesis 28:10-22 *(in groups or aloud)*. Then ask:

★ What happened to Jacob, and why was this experience special to him?

★ How did Jacob react to this experience?

★ What did Jacob do to mark the place as a holy site?

★ Why did Jacob call the place Bethel *(the house of God)*?

The Prison

Begin the session with two questions:

★ Can you think of a time when you felt out of control or lost?

★ What was the worst experience that you have had? Why?

Read Genesis 39:19-40:23 *(in groups or aloud)*. Then ask:

★ While Joseph was in prison, how did he experience the blessing or support of God?

★ What special help did God provide for Joseph?

★ How did God use people to help Joseph?

★ What gifts did Joseph have that might have helped him in his predicament?

★ Because of this experience, what might Joseph have learned about God's presence?

★ How was Joseph changed through this experience?

End the session by inviting the youth to find a spot to pray and to meditate on these Bible stories. Or work together to mark a special spot and consecrate it to God, and close with a blessing or prayer at this location.

38. Camp David

(A retreat study of the life of King David)

An outdoor or retreat study that works well with teenagers is a look at the life of King David. This study has four components, featuring four phases and events in the king's life. You may choose to conduct this study in a single session, or over the course of a weekend retreat. You will need Bibles, paper, and pencils.

The Young David

Begin the study by asking two questions:

★ What are the greatest challenges you have faced?
★ How did God help you meet these challenges?

Read 1 Samuel 17:38-54 *(in groups or aloud).*

Divide the youth into small groups, and invite them to list any insights they gained during the Scripture reading. Ask each group to comment on some of their insights. Then ask:

★ What made God's power so decisive in this story?
★ Why, do you think, did God pick a young boy to do this difficult job?
★ What responses did you hear or see that brought people closer to God?
★ What might God have been preparing David to become?

David the King

Read 2 Samuel 7 *(in groups or aloud)*. Then ask:

☆ What did David want to do for God?
☆ Have you ever wanted to do something special for God?
☆ What had God done for David?
☆ What has God done for you?
☆ What did David pray?
☆ If you were to compose a prayer today, what would it include? *(Distribute paper and pencils, and invite the youth to write a prayer. The youth may use David's prayer [verses 18-29] as a guide.)*

David's Great Sin

Read 2 Samuel 11:1-27 *(in groups or aloud)*. Then ask:

☆ What sins did David commit against God?
☆ How did David's sin with Bathsheba lead him to commit other sins?
☆ How does sin keep us from thinking about others? about God?

David's Restoration and Forgiveness

Read 2 Samuel 12:1-15 *(in groups or aloud)*. Then ask:

☆ How did God seek David in spite of his sin?
☆ How did God use people to bring David into a right relationship again?
☆ What changes did David make to show that he was sorry for his sin?
☆ How would you describe the changes that took place in David from his early years until this time in his life?
☆ In what ways is David's life a tribute to God's grace?
☆ What did you learn from David's life that can help you know God?
☆ What might God be saying to us today through these accounts of David's life?

39. Someone's Missing

(A study for helping teenagers mourn the death of a friend)

Provide Bibles, stationery, and ink pens for this study. Gather the youth (as well as any parents or adults who are participating), and open with a time of silence and prayer. This prayer time might also include a reading of Psalm 23.

Read Ecclesiastes 3:1-8 aloud. Then ask:

☆ Do you find the words of Ecclesiastes comforting or challenging? Why?

☆ Why, do you think, are so many hurtful and sad times mentioned in this Bible passage?

☆ Can you think of other sad times that are not mentioned in this passage?

Read John 14:1-4 and 16:20-24 aloud. Then ask:

☆ How do the words of Jesus comfort us in our loss today?

☆ What promises does Jesus give us?

☆ How does Jesus promise to help us with our pain and sorrow?

☆ How does Jesus challenge us to live?

In closing, distribute stationery and pens. Invite the participants to write letters of appreciation for things they admired about their friend who has died. If you like, the letters can be collected and read by the group members; or, if you prefer, mail the letters to the friend's family as keepsakes and expressions of love. Let the participants know what the plans are for the letters as they are writing them.

40. Pathways to Peace

(A study of the peace of God)

The Hebrew word *Shalom* is filled with rich meanings. Translations of this word can include *wholeness, completeness, reconciliation,* and *peace*. This study will help the youth experience this peace in their relationships, their personal lives, and with God. The sessions may be completed during a retreat or used as a three- to six-week study in youth group meetings.

Provide Bibles, modeling clay, paper, and pencils for this study.

Peace With God

Key Verse: "Therefore, since we are justified by faith, we have peace with God through our Lord Jesus Christ" (Romans 5:1).

Begin the session by asking the youth to close their eyes. Tell them that you are going to say a word, after which they are to recall the first image that pops into their minds. Say the word *peace*. Invite several youth to tell the group what came to mind when they heard the word *peace*.

Read Romans 5:1-21 *(in groups or aloud)*. Then ask:

☆ What is the image of peace that is presented in this passage?
☆ What argument is being made for having peace with God?
☆ How do we know that we have peace with God?
☆ What words are used to describe this peace we have with God?

Follow this discussion by inviting the youth to pray for peace with God. Then close by repeating in unison several times the Key Verse (Romans 5:1).

Peace With Others

Key Verse: "First be reconciled to your brother or sister, and then come offer your gift [to God]" (Matthew 5:24).

Give a small block of modeling clay to each person. Invite the youth to work together as a large group or in small groups to create a work of art that illustrates the power of peace with others.

Follow up by asking the participants to explain their artwork. If possible, display the artwork for a number of weeks in the youth room. Recite the Key Verse in unison, then read aloud **Matthew 5:22-24** and **Matthew 5:38-48.** Ask:

- ✮ What images of peace does Jesus offer in these teachings?
- ✮ How practical are some of these ideas?
- ✮ What makes peace with others challenging?
- ✮ What would happen if everyone lived by these teachings?
- ✮ How have you seen people living out these teachings today?
- ✮ Why is seeking peace with others often more difficult than seeking peace with God?

Peace With Yourself

Key Verse: "Do not let your hearts be troubled" (John 14:1).

Distribute paper and pencils. Invite the youth to make a top ten list of what they like most about themselves (humorous items as well as serious ones are allowed). Invite volunteers to read their list to the group.

Follow up by asking:

⭐ Why is it often difficult to talk about ourselves?
⭐ In what ways is it sometimes difficult to like ourselves?
⭐ What are some challenges a person might face if he or she is to experience personal peace?

Read in unison the Key Verse and **John 15:1-11.** Ask:

⭐ How can this passage help us have true joy and personal peace?
⭐ Why, do you think, is it often difficult to have joy?
⭐ How might we live in such a way that others can see that we are at peace?
⭐ What helps you be more peaceful?
⭐ How does God give you peace of mind?

Close with a prayer and the reading of **Psalm 23.**

Show Me the Way

PART FOUR

Bible Talks & More

Every good Bible teacher needs a few talks and presentations to help bring the Scriptures to life. Sometimes a simple speech or object lesson can light a fire in the minds of teenagers, giving them confidence that they can find help through the Bible.

Likewise, many opportunities are available to help teenagers memorize the Scriptures. You may have heard the saying, "The only Bible we really own is not the Bible we hold in our hands but the Bible we have in our hearts." Learning the Bible and committing it to memory can be a source of lifelong help.

This final section of the book will offer youth leaders and teachers an abundant source of practical talks and memorization techniques that they can use with little or no preparation.

Show Me the Way

41. People of the Book

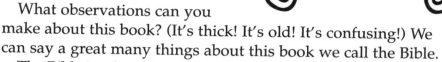

Theme: Learning the Bible
Supplies: a Bible

The Talk: (*Hold up a Bible.*)

What observations can you make about this book? (It's thick! It's old! It's confusing!) We can say a great many things about this book we call the Bible.

The Bible is a huge book. Or more accurately, it's a collection of books—66 in all. It's a book that has been around for centuries. It is also a book that takes a lifetime to know and understand—and even then, we will never know everything about the Bible.

But the Bible is also a special book. Christians have sometimes been called "people of the book." The reason is that Christians have always understood that the Bible is most important for our understanding of God, for our growth in faith, and for our understanding of how we are to live. The Bible is our most important book for all these reasons and more.

Keep in mind that the Bible can best be appreciated by following three simple guidelines. First, read the Bible. Many people own a Bible, but most Bibles are never read. Even reading the Bible a little a day can make a difference in your life.

Second, study the Bible with others. When we discuss Bible passages with others, we can learn more of what the Bible means, not just what the Bible says. This is why people have studied the Bible together for years .

Third, when you grow in your understanding of the Bible, you can begin to pass along your understanding to someone else—someone younger than you or someone who is searching for life's answers. Being a people of the book can help us be a more knowledgeable church, understand one another, and grow in our love and peace with others.

42. Inside out

The Talk: (*After reading aloud the Scripture lesson, hold up a baseball cap that has been turned inside out.*)

Theme: Transformation
Supplies: A Bible,
a baseball cap
Scripture: Romans 12:2

Sometimes, in the late innings of a baseball game, a team will turn their baseball caps inside out. This is supposed to help the team rally from behind. A rally cap is a baseball superstition that is meant to transform the momentum of the game.

Although you and I can't change the momentum of life by turning our clothing inside out, we can transform life—our lives—by focusing our attention and desire on the things of God. When you and I give ourselves to God wholly and freely, God transforms our lives into something beautiful and new. In fact, not only our minds are transformed but also our will, our desire, and our values are changed.

God can begin to transform us from the inside out in many ways. Reading the Bible and meditating on the Scriptures is one way we can listen to God. Knowing what God wants of us and wants us to be is important.

We might even consider the Bible our rally cap. When we feel down and insignificant, we are sure to find some needed help in the Bible. When we feel sorrow or pain, promises are available to us.

Somewhere in the Bible, we can find just the right words to help us through a difficult situation or a challenging time. All we need to do is open our minds—and our Bibles.

43. The Light

The Talk: *(Darken the room and do the talk with the aid of a flashlight or a flame.)*

Theme: Guidance
Supplies: a flashlight
or a flame
Scripture: Psalm 119:105

Electrical power is one of those blessings we generally take for granted. We rarely think about turning on a light or getting the heat and power we need . . . until our electricity goes off. Then we immediately miss it. In essence, we couldn't have many modern conveniences at all if it were not for electricity. We expect it to be there when we need it.

We can forget that God's power and promises are there when we need them. The Bible is a record of God's interaction with human history—a history of a frail humanity and a great God of love. It is a record of the many ways God has used ordinary people to do extraordinary things.

God has promised to use you and me as well. We don't have to be in the dark about God's love and God's amazing grace. The light is available through the Bible, the story of God's work and forgiveness.

Sometimes when the world seems dark and dismal, we can find just the light we need through the Scriptures. Words of comfort and hope, of joy and triumph, abound. God will see us through.

Don't turn out the light on God. Use the Bible as a guide into the glorious light of God's promise for your life. Let the Bible be a lamp for your feet and a light to your path.

44. Feed the Greed

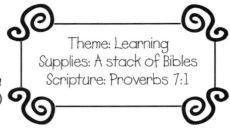

Theme: Learning
Supplies: A stack of Bibles
Scripture: Proverbs 7:1

The Talk: (*Place a stack of Bibles in front of the group to begin your talk.*)

Most of us would consider greed a negative and undesirable quality. We would probably say that we should be generous instead of greedy. We would say that it is more blessed to give than to hoard our possessions and desire more.

However, when it comes to the Bible, more is better—not necessarily having more Bibles, but knowing more about the Bible and learning more from the Bible. In the Book of Proverbs, we find this advice: "My child, keep my words and store up my commandments with you" (Proverbs 7:1).

When it comes to the knowledge of God, it doesn't hurt to be greedy. Having a desire to know more of God, to understand more about God, is a blessing. In fact, Jesus himself said that we should "seek first the kingdom."

A great many things can keep us from desiring more of God. We may become distracted by the quest for money, possessions, popularity, or even academic success. But when we keep our focus on the things of God, life works so much better.

Each of us can make a decision today to feed our greed for the priority of God's kingdom. We can choose to know more of God, spend more time with God, and learn to serve God's children—all through studying the Bible and talking about the Scriptures with other Christians. God bless us. And God grant us the desires of our hearts.

45. Bible Basics

The Talk:

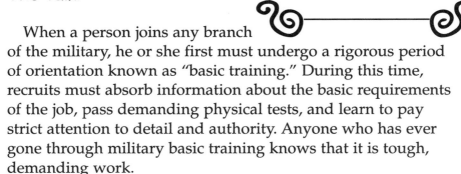

When a person joins any branch of the military, he or she first must undergo a rigorous period of orientation known as "basic training." During this time, recruits must absorb information about the basic requirements of the job, pass demanding physical tests, and learn to pay strict attention to detail and authority. Anyone who has ever gone through military basic training knows that it is tough, demanding work.

Growing in the Christian faith is also tough and demanding. Jesus once put the disciples through a period of basic training. He taught them. He demonstrated love by example. He gave the disciples opportunities for ministry. He sent them out to teach, love, and heal. Sometimes they failed. At other times, they succeeded.

We, too, are in a time of basic training. Jesus has offered us opportunities to serve and to help. And we can make the most of this time by having a guide or manual from which to learn what it means to be a disciple.

The Bible is our manual for basic training. In this guide we will find answers to questions about life, about God, about the hope of the world. We will also discover in the Bible how much God values us, how much we have to offer the kingdom of God, and how we can best serve others through our gifts and abilities.

The Bible is important to us because it contains instruction and wisdom and is a source of straight talk. So when you have questions, when you need answers, don't neglect the manual.

46. Proverbial Wisdom

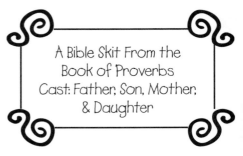

A Bible Skit From the Book of Proverbs
Cast: Father, Son, Mother, & Daughter

FATHER: Listen, children, to a father's instruction, and be attentive, that you may gain insight.

SON: I did not listen to the voice of my teachers or incline my ear to my instructors.

FATHER: Go to the ant, you lazybones; consider its ways, and be wise.

SON: Does not wisdom call, and does not understanding raise her voice?

FATHER: A wise child makes a glad father.

SON: The fear of the Lord is the beginning of wisdom.

FATHER: A soft answer turns away wrath, but a harsh word stirs up anger.

SON: To make an apt answer is a joy to anyone.

FATHER: The human mind plans the way, but the Lord directs the steps.

SON: How much better to get wisdom than gold!

MOTHER: And now, my children, listen to me: happy are those who keep my ways.

DAUGHTER: If you are wise, you are wise to yourself.

MOTHER: The foolish woman is loud; she is ignorant and knows nothing.

DAUGHTER: A gracious woman gets honor.

MOTHER: Like a gold ring in a pig's snout is a beautiful woman without good sense.

DAUGHTER: A generous person will be enriched, and one who gives water will get water.

MOTHER: The wise woman builds her house, but the foolish tears it down with her own hands.

DAUGHTER: Whoever is slow to anger has great understanding.

MOTHER: The eyes of the Lord are in every place.

DAUGHTER: The Lord has made everything for its purpose.

MOTHER: Better is a dry morsel with quiet than a house full of feasting and strife.

DAUGHTER & SON: House and wealth are inherited from parents.

MOTHER & FATHER: My child, if your heart is wise, my heart too will be glad.

47. Memory Cards

Youth should not be discouraged from trying to memorize portions of the Bible. In school, youth memorize algebraic formulas, spelling words, speeches, and sometimes even entire documents. Therefore, providing students with the ongoing challenge of memorizing Bible verses can also help them in the years ahead, when memorization becomes all important in higher education.

One quick way to assist youth in memorization is through the use of memory cards. When I was in college and was trying to learn Greek, I carried around vocabulary cards in my pocket all day long. Whenever I had a spare moment here or there, I pulled out the cards and learned a word or two. I memorized entire passages from *The Odyssey* in this way.

Distribute index cards (or small slips of paper) and ask the students to write on a card a favorite Bible passage. Invite them to carry this card with them throughout the week and try to have the verse or verses memorized by the following meeting.

Learning a verse or two each week in this fashion can enable a person to commit to memory a surprising number of Bible verses in a year's time.

48. Musical Memorization

Scientists and doctors have known for years now that each side of the human brain controls various functions, emotions, and actions of the body. We should not be surprised, then, to discover that not all people learn in the same fashion. Some people learn more readily by seeing (reading, observing, and so on). Others learn more readily by listening. Still others by doing.

Don't neglect that side of the brain that learns by hearing. In many ways, youth are most adept at learning through listening. Consider all of the song lyrics teenagers know by heart just from listening to a song a few times.

Use this knowledge of music to your teaching advantage. Many Bible verses can be easily memorized by employing music. Here's a simple technique:

Sit at a piano or use a background tape. Play music while reciting a Bible verse or verses to the music. Tunes as simple as "Chopsticks" can be used to teach a Bible verse quickly and easily. You can also use favorite pop songs or television theme songs.

Teenagers will have fun memorizing the Bible in this fashion. You might even find that the youth will create some new songs of their own—Bible verses set to music—that you can use in worship times or as a theme song for the group.

49. Verse of the Month

If your youth group uses a monthly or weekly newsletter, a bulletin board, or another source of communication, try adding a verse of the month (or a verse of the week) to encourage Bible memorization.

Many teenagers like the challenge of trying to memorize a Bible verse, especially if they know that others have accepted the same challenge. Start with giving the youth a few shorter verses, or stick with a particular theme. As the teens catch on, increase the length or number of verses.

At each youth meeting, reinforce the verse by reciting it aloud or asking for volunteers to recite it. Or encourage participation by having a Bible study around these weekly or monthly verses.

50. Learn by Acrostic

You have probably seen examples of Christian acrostics—word puzzles in which letters represent whole words or phrases. The Greek word for the Christian symbol of the fish (*Ichthus*) is an acrostic that means "Jesus Christ, Son [of] God, [the] Savior."

You can create your own acrostics as a way of helping youth memorize Bible verses or longer passages. For example, here is an alphabetical acrostic for the Beatitudes (found in Matthew 5:3-11). A similar acrostic concept is employed in the Hebrew Bible for Psalm 119. You can use the concept of the four *P*s, three *M*s, and an *H* to remember all the Beatitudes.

P Blessed are the **Poor** in spirit.

P Blessed are the **Pure** in heart.

P Blessed are the **Peacemakers**.

P Blessed are those who are **Persecuted** for righteousness' sake.

M Blessed are those who **Mourn**.

M Blessed are the **Meek**.

M Blessed are the **Merciful**.

H Blessed are those who **Hunger** and thirst for righteousness.

Show Me the Way